"ALONG CAME CANCER"

BY

VALERIE MORTIMER

COPYRIGHTS

DEDICATION

To Jim, Christopher and Ryan.

"Thank you for always lifting me higher."

CONTENTS

FOREWORD

Any diagnosis of cancer is imaginably overwhelming. Initially, it would help if you had time to absorb the information, but then you begin to have many questions and thoughts. Therefore, it is crucial to find suitable sources to obtain this information. We often lean on friends and family, research the internet, and read other experiences to find peace of mind. *Along Came Cancer* by Valerie Mortimer RN, MPA seeks to provide accurate real-life resources that apply to patients with any cancer diagnosis, not just metastatic breast cancer.

I have been treating oncology patients for over 25 years; it has always been my passion. I had devoted myself to the care of the oncology patient since the age of sixteen when I was the youngest hospice volunteer for a local hospital. Over the years, I have been blessed with having many wonderful experiences with both patients and families. However, it is much different when caring for one of your loved ones. Cancer has affected my family, witnessing my father succumb to the disease and not long after watching my mother conquer an extremely aggressive lung cancer only to have a different cancer three years later.

I reflected on the patient aspects of care, how much support families needed while going through this with a loved one, and how much went into preparing for a doctor's appointment with the oncologist. Being both the daughter and caregiver was not something easy to delineate. Although it was difficult, I now feel it has better helped me in my practice to truly empathize with what patients and families are facing.

Having this understanding of what patients go through when they leave the physician's office has enabled me to practice at a different level. As I stood beside my parents on their journey, I understood how patients feel and what they expect in a provider. My experience has given me the insight to provide the care that I would expect for my parents. The empathy I feel for my patients, and their loved ones have inspired me to provide unmatched care, which I try to deliver daily. To me, it is a privilege and an honor to be allowed to help patients through sometimes the most difficult time in their lives.

I have always practiced believing there is always something you can do. Whether curative, supportive, or palliative, you can always continue to support your patient.

I get to know the patient beyond the disease because the truth is there is so much more to them than a cancer diagnosis!

We all have the commonality of hope; in practice, I am amazed by the resilience of my patients; despite the struggles and constant ups and downs they face, the will to overcome supersedes cancer. The strength and gratitude remain as we see in *Along Came Cancer*. Drawing on her personal experiences from her nursing career, Valerie shapes her journey into a meaningful, enriching experience for others' benefit. It is a helpful and heartwarming book that discusses how her cancer journey has impacted her life. Despite setbacks and multiple chemotherapy lines, Valerie continues to be positive and live her life to the fullest. Being a patient and a nurse allows her to provide invaluable education to others going through a similar experience. Her words change your mindset and bring focus to living a good life despite a cancer diagnosis.

Part of what Valerie discusses is the emphasis on all elements of care. It validates the importance of supporting patients' physical, emotional, and spiritual elements of care and the importance of this as whole patient care. In addition, Valerie discusses not experiencing this alone and the importance of support, whether in the form of groups, family, or colleagues, giving way to the importance of commonality within each other.

This should be essential reading for anyone diagnosed with any type of cancer, as she provides expert advice that she has lived through! Despite all my years of oncology work, I never had a true understanding until it impacted me. You think you are prepared as a practitioner, but personally, it is a whole new experience. What Valerie displays in her book is her true experience and will be helpful for anyone with a cancer diagnosis.

INTRODUCTION

Two months after my 50th birthday, I was diagnosed with Stage 3 Intraductal Carcinoma of the Left Breast. The news didn't shock me completely. I had already been a Registered Nurse for 28 years and was well aware of how prevalent cancer was. What surprised me, though, was how little I knew about cancer and how much it would impact my life.

After working so many years in the healthcare field, it wasn't easy to go from being the one "in charge" to the person in the flimsy paper gown. It's still hard for me to sit on an exam table and "be" the patient. However, having the advantage of my medical background did help me make the transition a little easier.

No one likes to be blindsided, and hearing the words "You have cancer" is never easy. For most people, a cancer diagnosis comes as a complete surprise. It's often shocking. We're usually just going about our lives, and then cancer shows up.

It's never a good or convenient time to get cancer. And without access to decent medical care, health insurance, or a support system, it will be even more challenging.

I'm going to share a lot about cancer with you. I will educate you on the latest statistics and provide information from reputable sources. I will also share what I have learned from my first-hand experiences as a nurse for 35 years and a cancer patient for twelve. Of course, I feel most qualified to speak about breast cancer, but this book is for any cancer patient.

I have belonged to several cancer and wellness support groups for the past five years. Being a part of these groups has become a game changer for me. My fellow participants feel like they are my family members. We have taught one another a lot about how to survive and thrive with cancer!

Men and women of all different ages belong to these groups. We are diverse in the fact that we have differing religions, ethnicities, and socioeconomic and educational backgrounds. Due to the pandemic (and Zoom), these groups have expanded and cover a wider geographic area now as well. The single commonality throughout these groups is that the participants have all been, or still are, cancer patients.

Some of them were fortunate enough to have had what I like to call a "one and done" experience with cancer. Some have had several cancer journeys with either the same cancer reoccurring or a second or third type of cancer. Then there are those like me. We are living with ongoing cancer, which for now, is incurable.

In 2016, after enjoying five years living as what I thought was cancer free, I was diagnosed with Metastatic Breast Cancer (MBC). MBC is also known as Stage 4 breast cancer. With this diagnosis, I thought for sure I wouldn't live to see my 60th birthday. I did not picture myself being able to have a good quality of life. Thankfully I was wrong.

I am not saying that having cancer in any way is easy, but I will say cancer really has taught me some meaningful things. First, it has enabled me to live each day with purpose. It has shown me how capable and truly loved I am. But, most importantly, I have learned to live mindfully instead of living with a full mind.

Since the beginning of my cancer journey, I've been sharing my story with others. I started with my close circle and then expanded to a larger audience. I am amazed by how many times people comment that I am brave. I appreciate their sentiment, but I don't consider myself brave. Instead, I would say that I am strong, confident, and someone who wants to keep living.

Many wonderful things have happened to me throughout my life. I've always made a conscious effort to be a very caring human being. I have taken my roles as a mom, wife, daughter, friend, and nurse very seriously. In an attempt to help others and as part of my legacy, I have now written this book. My greatest hope is that by sharing what I have learned from my cancer journey and the journeys of others, it will help you with yours.

CHAPTER 1 –

KNOWLEDGE IS POWER

Upon hearing of a new cancer diagnosis, people experience a wide range of reactions and emotions. I would say from what I have witnessed, most people are usually surprised by it. Lots of time, they admit they are frightened and often angry too. For some, it takes a long time to process, and they have difficulty moving forward. Others want to learn everything possible about their new disease and be 100% in full control of how they are going to treat it. However you are going to proceed, it is best to arm yourself with as much knowledge as possible and then find the right professional(s) to partner with.

The word "cancer" refers to any of the 200 different diseases affecting many parts of the body that are characterized by the uncontrolled growth of cells that invade and damage the body's normal tissues. Cancer can begin in organ tissues, skin, bone, cartilage, fat, muscle, blood vessels, immune system, and bone marrow. These cells can form tumors, although not all cancers do. In addition, cancer cells sometimes spread from their original site to other places in the body via the bloodstream or lymphatic system.

According to the American Cancer Society, here are three common cancer facts. In the United States, one in three people will be diagnosed with cancer in their lifetime, and there is a 1-in-8 or 13% chance a woman will develop breast cancer. In addition, one in 23 men and one in 25 women will get colorectal cancer. That is a lot of cancer!

According to data collected by the National Cancer Institute, here are the estimated numbers of new cases for the top thirteen cancers in 2021 in the United States:

Breast	284, 200
Prostate	248,530
Lung	235, 760
Colon/rectal	149,500
Melanoma	106,110
Bladder	83, 730
Non-Hodgkin Lymphoma	81,560
Kidney	76,080
Endometrial	66,570
Leukemia	61,090
Pancreatic	60.43
Thyroid	44,280
Liver	42,230

I think it's good to have a perspective of what types of cancer occur most often, along with how common they actually are. Possibly for some, it helps soften the blow, but what's even more helpful to know is that having cancer is not usually a death sentence.

The risk of dying from cancer in the United States has decreased over the past 28 years, according to annual statistics reported by the American Cancer Society (ACS) on January 12, 2022. The cancer death rate fell 32% from its peak in 1991 to 2019, the most recent year for which data were available. The 32% drop in the cancer death rate between 1991 and 2019 translates to almost 3.5 million fewer cancer deaths during these years than what would have been expected if the death rate had not fallen. This success is largely because of fewer people smoking, combination treatments for many cancers, and prevention and early detection through screening for some cancers, including cancer in the breast, cervix, colon, prostate, rectum, and, more recently, lung. [1]

As for that 1-in-8 breast cancer chance statistic, it is helpful to know that more than 3.8 million breast cancer survivors are currently in the country, including women still being treated and those who have completed treatment. When I was originally diagnosed with breast cancer in 2010, I was sure I wouldn't get to live a long time. I thought that again when I was re-diagnosed in 2016. It's now 2022, and I'm still here!

Being diagnosed with breast cancer did catch me slightly off guard because no one in my family had ever had breast cancer. We did have a history of other cancers, but breast cancer was not one of them. Some types of cancers are more prevalent in certain families, but only 5-10 percent of cancers are clearly linked to the genes we inherit from our parents.

---

[1] American Cancer Society, "Risk of Dying from Cancer Continues to Drop at an Accelerated Pace," January 12, 2022, https://www.cancer.org/latest-news/facts-and-figures-2022.html

Sometimes our inherited genes are found to contain mutations that make cells more likely to divide and change rapidly, which can lead to cancer. For example, mutations in the BRCA2 gene are associated with an increased risk of breast cancer in men and women, as well as several other types of cancers like prostate cancer and pancreatic cancer.

In my husband's family, some members have Lynch Syndrome, which puts them at an increased risk of certain cancers such as stomach, small intestine, liver, gallbladder ducts, urinary tract, brain, and skin. Additionally, women with this disorder have a higher risk of developing cancer of the ovaries and lining of the uterus.

Cancer can form in these parts of the body when someone has this inherited condition because the mutations affect DNA mismatch repair. The mutations in these genes keep them from working properly. Not everyone who has these mutations will end up with cancer.

We didn't have this kind of "inside" knowledge years ago. If someone knows genetic mutations run in their family, they should get tested to see if they also carry the gene defects. If they do, they will need to be super vigilant about cancer prevention, screenings, and monitoring.

Of course, the best way to deal with cancer is not to get it in the first place. I will be discussing this at length in Chapter 4. However, in most cases, when cancer is detected earlier, it is easier to treat.

Cancer can be detected in several ways. Sometimes it is found during routine screening tests like colonoscopies, mammograms, and pap smears, which is why these screenings are so important. Sometimes cancer is found incidentally, like when a patient gets an x-ray and blood work as part of a workup or while being seen in the Emergency Room for a different problem. Often patients present to their health care providers with symptoms they are experiencing, like a painless lump, pain, or a change in what is usually the "norm" for them.

Typically biopsies, lab work, and radiological scans are indicated when cancer or a cancer reoccurrence is suspected. Once treatments begin, patients will require more scans and lab tests to monitor the treatments' effectiveness and the cancer status.

After cancer treatments are completed, many patients will continue to be followed to ensure their cancer has not returned. Those of us who have already spent some time in cancer "trenches" are very familiar with the feeling of "scanxiety." This is that anxious feeling we experience every time we have to have a scan and wait for the results!

How much it has grown and spread when cancer is initially diagnosed must be determined. Stages classify most cancers. Staging is done by evaluating cell samples from the abnormal, lumped cluster of cells. They are grouped into 4 stages of cancer. The first 2 stages are also called the early stages, while 3 and 4 are the later stages. The stages describe the extent of the progression or growth of the malignant tumor inside your body. Subtypes and subgroups will further classify certain cancers.

Through a blood sample, biomarker testing is a way to look for genes, proteins, and other substances such as biomarkers or tumor markers that can provide information about patients' cancer. Biomarker testing may also be referred to as tumor testing or tumor genetic testing, or genomic or molecular profiling. It shows what the tumor is made of. Biomarker tests are not the same as genetic testing.

All the available information is extremely important to know about your cancer to receive the best treatment. However, it's also important to remember your cancer is specific to you and your body. For example, one patient's lung cancer treatment may differ entirely from another patient's because they have a different type, location, severity, or amount of lung cancer.

There are several ways cancer can be treated depending on what type of cancer it is, how advanced it is, what patients will accept (and can afford), and what the goals of the treatment are.

Conventional cancer treatment options include surgery, chemotherapy, radiation therapy, targeted therapy, immunotherapy, hormone therapy, phototherapy, or stem cell or bone marrow transplants. These options are specific to the type and extent of cancer. Treatment combinations are often used, and they all have their own pros and cons. Some people choose to have no treatments at all for their cancer and just manage the symptoms. Others chose alternative options or a combination of conventional and alternative treatments.

Sometimes loved ones won't agree with your cancer treatment choices and may pressure you to select a different one. Some patients I've known preferred to have others make the decisions for them.

I assure you that most of the "cancer" decisions you will need to make are very difficult. It can be daunting if you're not a medical person, or even if you are. So my advice to you is to do all of your research and don't feel guilty about consulting with multiple medical professionals.

Most insurance plans do cover second opinions. These opinions can help empower patients with knowledge about their options and give them confidence in the proposed treatment plan. Once you've decided about your treatment(s), go forward confidently with your plan.

Now let's begin with surgery. Even the decision to proceed with surgical removal of one's cancer can be complicated when there are options. Once I learned my breast lump was cancerous, I was told I would need to have what I call the "hat trick" of cancer treatments (surgery, chemo, and radiation). A "hat trick" is when the same player scores three goals in a single hockey or soccer game – It's a major feat. I wasn't happy having any one of these treatments, no less all three!

My breast surgeon explained my surgical options to me. I could have just the lump removed (lumpectomy) or my full breast removed (mastectomy). She also told me I could "elect" to have my other breast removed as a precautionary measure.

She further explained my breast reconstruction options should I choose to have a mastectomy. I remember leaving her office very confused, thinking to myself that I did not want to be responsible for that kind of decision. After all, she was the doctor, and I was "just the patient." But then again, maybe I was fortunate to have options. I certainly didn't want to go through breast cancer again, so I underwent a double mastectomy with breast reconstruction. It certainly wasn't an easy decision to make or an easy surgical undertaking to go through.

Recently, a friend of mine was diagnosed with kidney cancer and called me for advice. After seeing a surgeon, he had the option of having his whole kidney removed or just the tumor. He told me he felt like he had left the doctor's office with so many unanswered questions. I encouraged him to write down his questions and then contact the doctor to get them answered.

I also let him know that getting a second, and maybe even a third, opinion would not hurt. After all, these are really big decisions we are being asked to make. At times not all of our cancer questions will have answers, but we can only go forward with the knowledge we have at the time. Finally, I reminded him that once he made his decision, he needed to remain confident in his choice.

Regarding chemotherapy for cancer treatment, I think it is the number one thing that comes to people's minds when they think of how cancer is treated. There are several reasons for using chemotherapy. Chemotherapy uses drugs to kill cancer cells by attacking dividing cells. Curative therapy aims to kill all cancer cells. Adjuvant therapy targets cells left after surgery to prevent recurrences. Neoadjuvant therapy is used to shrink tumors before surgery, and palliative therapy is to give relief when removing all of a patient's tumor cells is not possible.

Some types of chemotherapy damage the genetic code inside the cell that tells it how to copy or repair itself. Other types block chemicals the cells need to divide. Some normal cells in the body divide often, such as hair and skin cells, so these cells sometimes end up being killed by the chemo. This is why hair loss occurs with some chemotherapies. [2]

There are over 100 different chemotherapy drugs. They are classified according to their chemical nature and function. Some well-known cancer chemotherapy agents

---

[2] Medline Plus NIH National Library of Medicine, "Cancer Chemotherapy", accessed March 22, 2022, https://medlineplus.gov/cancerchemotherapy.html

include alkylating agents, plant alkaloids, antimetabolites, anthracyclines, topoisomerase inhibitors, and corticosteroids. The types are used to treat different cancers and have different side effects. These agents can be administered orally, by injection, or intravenously. Chemotherapy treatments are systemic, which means healthy cells in the body are also attacked.

Radiation therapy for cancers uses high-energy particles or waves to destroy or damage cancer cells, thereby shrinking tumors. Radiation works by making small breaks in the DNA inside cells. These breaks keep cancer cells from growing and dividing and cause them to die. Nearby normal cells can also be affected by radiation, but most recover and return to working as they should. The treatments are usually aimed at and affect only the part of the body needing treatment. [3]

Radiation can be administered either externally, internally, or systemically. Internal radiation is also called brachytherapy. In brachytherapy, a radioactive source is put directly inside the body, into or near the tumor, and left there.

---

[3] American Cancer Society, "How Radiation Therapy Is Used to Treat Cancer", accessed March 23, 2022,
https://www.cancer.org/treatment/treatments-and-side-effects/treatment-types/radiation/basics.html

With systemic radiation, drugs are given by mouth or injected into a vein. [4]

Targeted therapy like chemotherapy is used to attack cancer cells, but these drugs target the changes in cancer cells that help them grow, divide and spread. Different types of cancer cells have different gene changes and proteins, or enzymes that send messages to tell the cancer cell to grow and replicate. Targeted therapies target the proteins to block the messages, causing the cancer cells to stop growing or destroy themselves. Targeted therapy is less toxic to healthy cells than chemo, but side effects can also occur with these drugs.

Targeted cancer therapies are sometimes called molecularly targeted drugs/therapies or precision medicines. Precision medicine is a form of medicine that uses information about a person's genes and proteins to prevent, diagnose and treat disease. [5]

---

[4] American Cancer Society, "How Radiation Therapy Is Used to Treat Cancer", accessed March 23, 2022, https://www.cancer.org/treatment/treatments-and-side-effects/treatment-types/radiation/basics.html

[5] NIH National Cancer Institute, "Targeted Therapy to Treat Cancer", accessed March 23, 2022, https://www.cancer.gov/about-cancer/treatment/types/targeted-therapies

Immunotherapy is a type of cancer treatment that assists the immune system fight to cancer. The immune system helps your body fight infections and other diseases. It comprises white blood cells, organs, and tissues of the lymph system. Immunotherapy is a type of biological therapy. Biological therapy is a type of treatment that uses substances made from living organisms to treat cancer. Several types of immunotherapy to treat cancer include: immune checkpoint inhibitors, T-cell transfer therapy, and monoclonal antibodies.[6]

Photodynamic therapy uses a drug activated by light, called a photosensitizer or photosensitizing agent, to kill cancer or precancerous cells. The light can come from a laser or other source. Photodynamic therapy is often used as a local treatment to treat a specific body part. Photodynamic therapy limits damage to healthy cells outside of the treatment area. Still, because the light can only penetrate a thin layer of tissue, it can't reach far into large tumors.[7]

---

[6] NIH National Cancer Institute, "Immunotherapy to Treat Cancer", accessed March 24, 2022, https://www.cancer.gov/about-cancer/treatment/types/immunotherapy

[7] NIH National Cancer Institute, "Photodynamic Therapy to Treat Cancer", accessed March 25, 2022, https://www.cancer.gov/about-cancer/treatment/types/photodynamic-therapy

A bone marrow transplant is also called a stem cell transplant or, more specifically, a hematopoietic stem cell transplant. Transplantation can be used to treat certain types of cancer such as leukemia, myeloma and lymphoma, and other blood and immune system diseases that affect the bone marrow.

Stem cells are special cells that make copies of themselves and then change into the different kinds of blood cells the body needs. When stem cells are damaged, they may not form the necessary amounts of red blood cells, white blood cells, or platelets. Without this, our immune system can no longer fight the viruses and bacteria that make us sick, blood may not clot properly, and oxygen won't be effectively carried throughout our body.

When healthy stem cells or bone marrow is successfully transplanted into patients' bones or blood, the ability of the body to create the necessary red and white blood cells and platelets is restored. If cancer treatments are going to cause damage to stem cells, they will be removed before the treatment begins and returned to the patient's body after the treatment is completed. This is known as an auto transplant or stem cell rescue.

In allogeneic transplants, stem cells come from another person, a donor. A donor match must be a healthy person whose blood proteins closely match the patients. Siblings from the same parents are often the best match, but another family member or an unrelated volunteer can be a match too. [8]

Hormone therapy is a treatment that slows or stops the growth of breast, prostate, endometrial and adrenal cancers since certain hormones enable some cancers to grow. Cancer growth can be slowed down or stopped by blocking or altering the hormones. Most types of hormone therapy are drugs taken by mouth. Some are given by injection. Some types of surgery can be considered a form of hormone therapy, like removing the testicles in men or the ovaries in women.

I have just provided you with a few general cancer statistics in an attempt to show you how prevalent cancer is. I have also given you a brief explanation of the available conventional cancer treatment options out there. Now I think

---

[8] Cancer.Net, "What is a Bone Marrow Transplant (Stem Cell Transplant)?", accessed March 26, 2022, https://www.cancer.net/navigating-cancer-care/how-cancer-treated/bone-marrowstem-cell-transplantation/what-bone-marrow-transplant-stem-cell-transplant

it's important to move on to discussing what a cancer prognosis is and how they are determined.

A prognosis is a doctor's estimate of a disease's likely course and potential outcome. For example, the prognosis of a patient diagnosed with cancer is often viewed as the chance that the disease will be treated successfully and that the patient will recover. However, these statistics vary based on the type of cancer, the stage of cancer, the age, and the overall health condition of the patient.

Prognosis is determined by your doctor, who bases their assessment, in part, on information researchers have collected over many years on hundreds and sometimes thousands of people with the same cancer. The most commonly used statistics to determine patients' prognosis are cancer-specific survival rates, relative survival rates, overall survival rates, and disease-free survival rates, which can be broken down by type (and subtypes) of cancer, age groups, gender, and ethnicity.

Cancer survival statistics are often given regarding a 5-year survival relative to the general population. However, since survival statistics are based on large groups, they cannot be used to predict what will happen to individual patients. Also, because it takes years to see the impact of new treatment and diagnostic tests, the statistics a doctor uses to make a prognosis may not reflect the effectiveness of current treatments. [9]

I am someone who has a love/hate relationship with statistics. In graduate school, a statistics class was a requirement for my degree. Words like mean, median, mode, bell curves, standard deviations, and statistical significance represented concepts that hurt my head back then and still do. I barely passed this class.

On a personal level, although I find statistics confusing and difficult to comprehend, I truly do understand their importance. In my opinion, however, one should never put their full credence into disease statistics because they are based on complex individual human beings who are not the same as inanimate objects.

When quantifying humans' "health," there are a lot of gray areas. Not all patients react like the majority of the other patients. Statistics have outliers. If it is estimated that 1 in every 100 patients in the United States having surgery will get a surgical site infection, and you're the patient who gets

---

[9] Cancer Therapy Advisor, "Understanding a Cancer Prognosis", accessed April 2, 2022
https://www.cancertherapyadvisor.com/home/tools/fact-sheets/understanding-a-cancer

one, isn't that 100 percent for you? It is great to have a general consensus you can compare yourself to but remember, out there in this big world; there is only one you!

CHAPTER 2 – TAKING THE WHEEL

I was a good patient when I went through breast cancer treatment for the first time. However, I didn't take the news well when I was informed about my metastatic breast cancer six years later. I was angry. With my first cancer, I endured an extremely rough year. I did everything as per the doctor's and scientific recommendations. I had a double mastectomy, chemotherapy, and radiation sessions, which were all challenging for me in their own way for the complexity they carry for first-time patients. I believed these interventions would allow me to put breast cancer in the review mirror. I didn't think about it, even for a second, that I needed to be watching over my shoulder for its return.

When it was determined that my original breast cancer was found in my bones, my diagnosis was upgraded to stage 4 metastatic breast cancer. Currently, there is no cure for this cancer, only treatments that can prevent it from spreading. I decided I was not leaving anything up to chance in this new fight.

I was determined to become and remain an extremely informed consumer. I was starting a second cancer journey, but with my life at stake this time. I knew I would need to be 100 percent vested in all my cancer decisions. For my cancer information, I turned to three different places: my doctor, credible cancer resources and the cancer community.

After discovering my breast lump in 2010, I called my gynecologist immediately. He sent me for a mammogram, which confirmed the lump was suspicious and that I would need a biopsy. He gave me the name of a breast cancer surgeon. She performed a biopsy, and once she had the results, she informed me that I would need to "find" an oncologist. She said she had the names of some oncologists that she could refer me to. I took them from her, but I went home and immediately reached out to every woman I knew with a breast cancer history. There were quite a few.

One of these women, whom I trusted a lot, suggested I use her oncologist, and she gave me her name. This doctor was affiliated with a renowned cancer center that was not geographically too far from me and was on my health insurance plan. These are the three primary considerations for many cancer patients.

Throughout my cancer journey, I have never thought, "Why me?" However, there have been times when I've gotten angry and felt sorry for myself. On those occasions, I force myself to recall all I have to be grateful for, and my oncologist truly is one of them. Not only is she highly competent, but she is also very compassionate. She listens and communicates very well too. So far, she has been my only oncologist on this journey, although to be on the safe side, I consulted with another one once. I was happy and relieved to hear that the consulting oncologist agreed with what I was doing. The fact that my oncologist was happy that I sought another oncologist's opinion made me respect her even more.

Be sure to remember this. Finding a doctor, you feel comfortable with is the best place to start. Make sure they answer your questions and listen to what you have to say. Before signing up for anything, you must fully understand what you are consenting to! Sometimes it's helpful to ask the doctor face-to-face about what they would do if they, or their loved ones, were in a similar situation.

The next bit of advice here is to be careful using "Dr. Google." A lot of information on the internet can be helpful, but there is also a lot of misleading, confusing, and false information that could misguide you. Many sites are promoting and selling unproven cancer therapies and remedies, and we can be a vulnerable population. Keep your searches to reputable websites. The American Cancer Society and the National Cancer Institute are two of my favorites.

Sometimes it may be challenging, but make sure you discuss with your doctor the information you've found or heard from other people. If you think it may be something that will be helpful to you, it's worth getting their opinion on. It's now time for you to speak up on behalf of yourself! If you don't feel comfortable doing this, make sure you bring someone to your doctor visits who can or look for another doctor.

I have included a list of cancer resources and communities at the back of this book. Some of them even offer financial assistance to patients. The list certainly isn't all-inclusive, but you can do your search or ask your providers and social workers in your cancer centers. They may also be able to provide you with information and names of organizations. If you can't find an in-person group to join, there are many available on social media. Although your "community" can be beneficial, it should not be the only place you get your information from.

Getting the support you need, finding a good health care team, and deciding on your treatment plan are all necessary. However, financial concerns are primary for many people, even with good support and medical care. We all wonder how much all of this will cost and what will happen if we have to stop working.

Currently, three federal laws are in place to provide some protections and benefits for people with cancer and their loved ones. They are the Americans with Disabilities Act (ADA), the Family and Medical Leave Act (FMLA), and the Vocational Rehabilitation Act of 1973. The governmental agency that oversees the enforcement of these laws is the equal opportunity commission (EEOC). If you have questions about workplace legal protections, the toll-free number is 800-669-4000.

Under the ADA, people with health problems, including cancer, are protected from discrimination. This applies to companies with 15 or more employees. The FMLA applies to companies with 50 or more employees and allows the person with cancer and family members to take up to 12 weeks of unpaid leave for a medical condition while still protecting their job. In addition, under the vocational rehabilitation act, people with cancer may be eligible for job retraining.

At this time, I feel it's important to mention this before I continue. I realize as I am telling you about all the things I've learned from my cancer journey and giving you advice we are all not the same. As I've talked about cancers being so individualized, so are our journeys. Some of us are more fortunate than others, not only if we have an easier, more treatable cancer but for other reasons. The saying, "We are all in the same storm, but we're not all in the same boat," is so appropriate here.

Weathering the storm in a fifty-foot cabin cruiser is not the same experience as enduring it in a rowboat without oars. I said in my introduction that people's cancer journeys would be more difficult without affordable, decent medical care, or for patients who can't access it. Some may not get to make confident choices. Some don't have friends and family to count on. I realize things are not equal for all of us, but I believe every reader will find something in this book that can help them make dealing with cancer a little easier. Please keep reading!

CHAPTER 3 – A PUNCH TO THE STOMACH AND A KICK TO THE HEAD

I find group meetings interesting when people are asked to speak about their cancer journeys. However, everyone's story is uniquely their own. I always notice a few common themes. People say it was a bizarre experience while they were going through it. They often express their initial reaction that they thought their life would end and wondered how their families would go on without them. People often talk about how they just wanted things to appear like everything was "fine" while they were going through it and that they couldn't wait for things to return to "normal" after it was behind them.

Listening to the stories people with advancing, recurring, or incurable cancers tell is a little different for everyone. I often hear them say it's like being on one long roller coaster ride. They welcome the excitement that small victories bring. They're comfortable when they're just coasting but then anxiously holding their breath, knowing rough, uncertain patches are ahead. They all say grateful, hopeful, and challenging words when they tell their stories. I get that!

When I first felt that lump in my breast, I immediately thought I would throw up and pass out. Several years earlier, I had a problem with breast cysts, but this time I intuitively felt something was seriously wrong. When I learned of the diagnosis and what treating it entailed, I felt like I had been punched in the stomach. It was hard for me to catch my breath. I was so fearful that something was going wrong, and I couldn't fathom how life would turn out for my husband and two sons if I were no longer in the picture.

I felt embarrassed to let anyone know how afraid I was. After all, I was a grown woman and also a nurse. Nevertheless, I put on a brave face, continued working full time to be as distracted as possible, and delivered an excellent performance.

On January 6, 2011, I underwent a double mastectomy. First, the breast surgeon removed all of my breast tissue. Then, a plastic surgeon stepped in to begin the initial reconstructive phase. Unfortunately, the entire surgical reconstruction phase lasted another two years, encompassing five more surgeries and a nasty infection.

After the initial bilateral mastectomy and a few weeks of healing, I began the unpleasant experiences of my first round of chemotherapies. My therapy consisted of three drugs; Adriamycin, cisplatin, and Taxol, and it took four months to complete. I experienced complete hair loss, nausea, fatigue, and plenty of aches and pains on these drugs.

More recently, for most breast cancers, chemotherapy is now done before surgery. After chemotherapy, next on the list for me were radiation treatments to my left chest, 28 of them. These treatments were the first time I had participated in a clinical trial. I will discuss medical research and clinical trials in Chapter 5.

I worked full time and did my best to ensure everything continued as "normal." Unfortunately, I became progressively more fatigued during this time. I also sustained a painful 4x6 inch burn on my chest that took quite a bit to heal. Out of all 3 treatment modalities, radiation was my least favorite.

After surgery, chemo, and radiation were completed, there was still one more breast cancer-fighting option for me to consider. My breast cancer was and still is, fueled by estrogen, which meant hormone therapy was indicated.

I knew about the critical role estrogen plays in a woman's body. It was already bad enough that I had to sacrifice my breasts. However, I did consider myself lucky to be diagnosed later in life. Therefore, I didn't need to be concerned with bearing children and fertility issues. Since I didn't want to chance my cancer's return, I started hormone therapy.

The hormone issues here are complicated. I like to use an analogy that taking most of the estrogen out of a woman's body is like removing most of the water from your pet goldfish's bowl. (It's not a nice thing to do.) As a result, some fallouts were mood swings, irritability, body aches, and low energy levels. But, of course, life was already complicated. Still, I was on a mission to be "one and done" with breast cancer. So, over the next five years, I swallowed a pill every day.

Okay, so that was my breast cancer story, Part One. It would have been awesome if the story ended there with the words, "And I've been cancer free ever since." But, of course, you already know that's not how it turned out for me, but good news here, lots of people's cancer stories do end like that! And since most of us love a story with a happy ending, please keep reading - I feel there is one in mine.

One Sunday in July 2016, my husband and I were in a yoga class. While moving out of a pose, I experienced sudden, excruciating back pain. That day, getting off the floor, into the car, and onto my living room couch was a monumental feat. After four days without any relief, I knew I had to see a doctor.

I scheduled an appointment with our orthopedist. I still remember that discerning look on his face as he examined me. He sent me for a bone scan which showed I had cancer in several places in my spine, ribs, right hip, pelvis, and left arm. This news was more traumatic than that original gut-wrenching, punch to the stomach, take your breath away feeling I had experienced six years earlier. This time it felt similar to that but with a kick to the head too. I knew my life would never be the same upon receiving this news. I cried for days.

With the bone scan results, my husband and I went to see my oncologist, who I had not seen for a while – remember, I thought I was cancer free. She felt it was probably the original breast cancer that showed up and recommended I have a bone biopsy done to confirm this. She also wanted me to have a PET scan to see if the cancer had spread to other places like my liver, lungs, or brain. I had been "fortunate" in two aspects, the biopsy confirmed it wasn't a new cancer, and the PET scan confirmed it was "only" in my bones. It was time to decide on a whole new treatment plan.

Many advanced cancers are incurable because they are resilient and can't be destroyed. The currently approved drugs only temporarily damage cancer, not wholly killing it. Eventually, the cancer cells figure out how to replicate despite the drug(s), and tumors start to grow again.

Sometimes the medication's side effects can become too much for a patient to tolerate, and their quality of life becomes negatively affected. It may be time to consider stopping the med or changing to a different one. When the drug stops working altogether, it needs to be discontinued.

After getting over my initial shock, I started doing a lot of thorough research. Then, with careful consideration, I started on "let's fight MBC drug #1." This was a daily oral medication known as a CDK4/6 inhibitor. It worked by interrupting the process through which breast cancer cells divide and multiply. The side effects weren't too harmful, but the drug stopped working after a few months.

I also needed to have radiation for the tumor in my hip. That tumor was big, and because of where it was located had the potential to cause a future problem. Of course, I didn't want to end up with a broken hip. Again, my experience with radiation resulted in a terrible burn. This time, on my right buttock.

When drug number one stopped working, it was on to drug number two. This was another type of targeted therapy, also in oral pill form. It was Mammalian target of rapamycin also known as mTOR inhibitor drug. These drugs act by inhibiting the cell cycle and preventing T-Cell proliferation. I had to stop taking it once it stopped working.

Drug number three was a medication being studied in a clinical trial. It was an oral medication, but because I was taking it as a part of the research protocol, there was a lot of vigorous testing and monitoring. It was grueling, but I was happy to be helping out science and future MBC patients like me. I was also hopeful it would work for me. Unfortunately, three months into the trial, they tested me. They realized I did not benefit from it, so the drug was discontinued. Next, we moved to drug number four.

Drug number four was oral chemotherapy, classified as an antineoplastic. I got a little mileage from this drug, and the side effects weren't too harmful. Eventually, though, that resilient cancer of mine started to regrow. In the summer of 2019, a scan showed the cancer was now in my liver.

At the onset of receiving my MBC diagnosis, I knew what I was in for. However, some of me didn't want to believe it would happen. My family and I were educated about what would eventually happen. Still, we were hopeful it wouldn't – I guess sometimes denial can be a good thing, mainly because we were having tons of fun living in the moment. For the most part, on most days, I had been feeling great.

After a few days of letting this new development settle in, I accepted it was a new reality. I decided to stay the course and continue with the fight. Now was the time for me to muster up more grit and determination. After all, I had cancer, but cancer didn't have me.

It was time to up the ante, and I was started on chemo drug number five. This one was in an intravenous (IV) form of a mitotic inhibitor. They work by interfering with the growth and spread of cancer cells. Unfortunately, infusions meant more frequent trips to the Cancer Center. It worked for a while but with complete hair loss as a side effect. I thought being bald once was difficult, but losing my hair the second time was more brutal.

Next up was drug number six. It was administered in IV form, also. It was a non taxane microtubule inhibitor. It needed to be stopped when I developed numbness and pain in my feet. This condition is called neuropathy and is a common side effect of chemotherapy. The peripheral nerves in the hands and feet can become affected. Not only was this side effect a painful one, but it made it difficult for me to walk. Thankfully when the drug was stopped, my neuropathy disappeared, which doesn't always happen.

Drug number seven was an IV chemo drug, which wasn't too bad. It was an antineoplastic cytotoxic antimetabolite. It worked for a few months, and I didn't experience any side effects.

Drug number 8 was a combination of daily oral meds and injections. The injections were a hormone therapy given once a month in both buttocks. These injections were very uncomfortable. The pills were CDK4/6 inhibitors and gave me awful diarrhea.

With the amount of diarrhea that came with this drug, I was relieved when it stopped working. I liked that it was in oral form, which meant it didn't tie me into consistent trips to the chemo suite but instead there were always frequent and urgent trips to the bathroom.

Drug number nine was some more of drug number six, the IV medication I had to stop taking because I developed neuropathy. I remember thinking I would be in a good spot if it had worked as well as it did the first time and the neuropathy didn't occur. It worked well this second time (for a few months), but after my first dose, all of my hair fell right out.

This was now the third time being a bald woman. I didn't like it when it happened to me the first time in 2011. It saddened me, but I understood why it occurred. The second time I was angry, I never thought I would experience baldness again. By the time I lost it the third time, I had just accepted and embraced that it had happened. It had grown back the previous two times, and I decided to be optimistic that it would eventually regrow again.

One of my favorite photos of myself was from 1982 when I was my college's homecoming queen. In this photo, I am wearing a white gown, holding a bouquet of red roses, with a tiara on my head. My hair back then was down to my waist, super thick, strong, and shiny. In a more recent photo of me that I adore, I have a bald head, my arms flexed, and a smile from ear to ear. All these years later, I've realized that I, not my hair, have strength. I fully understand that it's not our hair that makes us beautiful. To me, beauty has nothing to do with physical looks. It has everything to do with how we are as people and how we make others feel about themselves.

Presently I am on the tenth course of treatment for Metastatic Breast Cancer. (Really, only nine, if you're counting, since I was on the same drug twice.) The critical thing is...I'm still here!! I am feeling healthier than I've ever felt and keeping busier. This cancer ordeal has made me grow in ways I would never have thought was possible.

I didn't learn too much from the first part of my cancer journey, and that's okay. My goal was to successfully get through it and to put it behind me as quickly as possible. However, going through it the second time opened my eyes immensely. I woke up and started living my life with intentions instead of habit.

This quote I came across from the Dalai Lama helps demonstrate my point. He is the head monk of Tibetan Buddhism, and when asked what surprised him the most about humanity, this is how he answered. "Man sacrifices his health to make money. Then he sacrifices money to recuperate his health. And then he is so anxious about the future that he does not enjoy the present: the result being that he does not live in the present or the future: he lives as if he is never going to die, and then dies having never really lived."

CHAPTER 4 - THERE ARE NO GUARANTEES

I started this book by providing you with a little bit of cancer knowledge in regard to how prevalent it is, how the odds are favorable that it's not always the immediate death sentence we all fear, and also discussed current treatment methodologies. I then told you of the ways I chose to treat my cancer. Again, deciding how you are going to treat your cancer is a very personal choice.

When I wound up back in my oncologist's office five years after thinking I had beat cancer, I remember asking her why this happened, especially after all I had done to be a perfect patient. She responded by explaining that this is how advanced cancer works and that the medical treatments do not come with a guarantee. She actually used the words "crap-shoot" in this discussion too. Crap-shoot? Those of you not familiar with the dice game Craps, that's what it is...A dice game of chance. How could this be? No guarantees and chances? This is my life we were talking about!

Again, this very patient doctor explained to my husband and me that although there wasn't currently a cure for MBC, many treatments could be utilized to slow down the disease's progression. I was mad, but I considered this good news since I had options to try. It became apparent to me right there that I'd be stepping back into the ring to face cancer again. It was time for another fight, and I was determined to give it my best shot. This time though, I realized I would also need to employ some new strategies. I will be going into a lot of detail about them, but first, I need to bring up something that I have noticed is often confusing to many cancer patients.

In Chapter 1, I spoke about cancer prognosis. This is your doctor's best estimate of how cancer will affect you and how your cancer will respond to your treatment(s). As already discussed, it is very specific. The goals of a patient's cancer treatments are also something that is very specific and can change depending on where they are in their journey. Some patients' cancer treatment goals are for curative purposes or to prolong their survival. For some, the goal is for palliative purposes with a focus on improving quality of life, relieving symptoms, or preventing complications.

In early 2017, I noticed in my medical record that my oncologist had classified the goal of my therapy as "palliative." This, again, made me feel instantly sick to my stomach. I had come to terms with the fact that she was working with me and my incurable illness, but I thought classifying me as a "palliative care" patient was a way of saying my life was going to end soon. That was not the case.

Palliative care is not the same as hospice care. Both palliative care and hospice care provide comfort to incurable patients. But palliative care can begin at diagnosis and at the same time as treatment. Hospice care begins after treatment of the disease is stopped and when it is clear that the person is not going to survive the illness much longer.

Living the past six years with an incurable illness has been interesting, to say the least. I am grateful that the quality of my life has been pretty good, and I still remain hopeful. A Yiddish expression I heard years ago wraps it up perfectly for me. "When you must, you can!" And on the subject of guarantees, this is a favorite quote of mine by Jeffrey Moscoso. "There are only two things you are guaranteed in life, birth, and death. What you do in between is entirely up to you."

CHAPTER 5 – EATING HEALTHY

About a year ago, I watched a documentary called "The C-Word – We Can Beat Cancer Before It Beats Us." This award-winning documentary focuses on the bad choices we make and the bad habits we form. It was produced by filmmaker Meghan O'Hara and featured a French physician and neuroscientist named David Servan-Schreiber.

Dr. Servan-Schreiber was first diagnosed with brain cancer at the age of 31. He was treated twice for this malignant brain tumor and became a leading figure in integrative approaches for the prevention and treatment of cancer. I apologize for the spoiler alert. Dr. Servan-Shreiber died in 2011 of his cancer. He was an amazing human being, and I highly recommend this documentary. [10]

---

[10] "The C Word", documentary film by Meghan LaFrance O'Hara, executive produced by Morgan Freeman, 2015, Revelations Entertainment & Impact Partners.

As I watched this documentary, it really resonated with me. The doctor focused on four areas and the impact they have on cancer. Working in the healthcare field for so many years, I had already given a lot of thought to this already for all diseases. These areas were nutrition, exercise, avoiding toxins, and managing stress. Now I have a lot to say about these four areas from my own personal perspective.

I feel there are two other areas that should be included as well. They are the art of balance and the body, mind, and spirit connection. There is a lot of overlap among them, as you will see. Let's begin with nutrition.

I grew up in the suburbs of Long Island, New York. My childhood was really nice. There was me, my older sister, and my younger brother, raised by our mother and father. My dad worked in Manhattan, and my mother was a stay-at-home mom. My mom cooked for us nightly, and although she didn't make fancy, gourmet meals, she fed us well. For dinner, the portions were not too big, and we ate a meat serving, a vegetable serving, and a starch serving. Dessert was usually canned fruit or pudding. (Of course, we also ate breakfast and lunch!) We usually didn't have snacks in our house. It was the sixties and seventies, and most people we knew didn't really either. Snacks were for holidays or when "company" was coming over. Unexciting but fairly healthy is how I would explain my diet in my younger years.

Next came four years of college. This was the first time I lived away from home and really got to exercise my own choices. It also began my years of eating poorly. I quickly discovered how much I loved Doritos, Oreos, and Pop-Tarts and how conveniently they could fill in for any missed meal. When I did go for a meal in the campus cafeteria, I ate all of the wrong things. I wasn't someone who went to college and gained the "freshman 10," but I did not make good food choices.

By the time I became a nurse, I was always so busy I pretty much existed on junk food and lots of caffeine. As a healthcare professional, I knew what good nutrition was and often educated my patients about it. I was definitely "a do as I say and not as I do" person when it came to that.

When my husband and I first started dating, the only two things I knew how to cook were fried, breaded chicken cutlets and fettuccini alfredo. He was impressed, I think, the first few times I served it to him, but after a while, I knew I'd have to expand my repertoire. I started making better quality meals for him, but my preference was still for unhealthy food.

This similar scenario continued once we had children. From the onset of their lives, I made sure they were properly nourished. I tried to ensure they ate according to that food pyramid and its corresponding recommendations. For myself, I continued ignoring that food model and continued on the "eating poorly" train. Upon originally learning I had breast cancer, it immediately occurred to me that maybe my 30 years of very bad eating habits were an awful idea.

At my visit with my oncologist, hearing that I now had MBC, I remarked that I should have eaten better because I probably wouldn't have gotten cancer again. Her reply was so on point when she told me it was impossible to travel back in time to undo things I'd already done. All I could do was move forward with the knowledge I had today. She also told me that it would serve no purpose to beat myself up for things I'd done in my past.

Wow – read those three lines again if you need to – They are so profound. How fortunate was I to receive this wisdom from such an intelligent woman who became my doctor because I had cancer? Apparently, this really resonated with me because I stopped beating myself up right after that visit. I started seeing a nutritionist, and I started eating a whole bunch better too!

I know eating all of the time properly will not guarantee that people will never become ill, but I know it helps when we stack the deck in our favor. Of course, there are always those outliers that we all know. Those people who have such unhealthy lifestyles and yet they remain disease free and, conversely, those who do all of the "right things" and still end up getting sick.

I'm not fully convinced yet that there is a perfect cancer prevention diet out there or one that actually cures cancer. I can tell you this, though; most of the time, eating a healthy diet will benefit you immensely. It will enable you to stay healthier longer and give you much more energy than eating poorly. Along with feeling better, it makes you look better too.

When you are healthy, it shows. Think of the people you know right now who eat healthy consistently. Don't they always have such nice skin and healthy-looking hair? My hair, when I have it on my head, is very healthy hair. Even with all of the toxins that I put in my body via these chemotherapeutic drugs, my skin has never looked nicer. I truly believe all of the fruits, greens, and healthy grains I eat, along with only minimal amounts of alcohol, processed food, and sugar, really make a difference.

In a way, now the food I eat has become like my medicine. I am very aware of what I put into my body. Remember when I said cancer woke me up and I switched from living by habit to intention? It's a choice I've made, and I certainly don't regret it. I don't want to eat kale and carrots, and of course, I would still prefer cheesecake over a serving of broccoli, but now I seriously think about my choices.

It's important to me that I am honoring my body. It will not cure my cancer at this point, but it can prevent other illnesses and helps with my energy levels. It sometimes is a fine line, though, here. Eating healthy is one of the ways to care for ourselves, but doing what makes us happy is also so important.

Comfort food is called comfort food because it's comforting. Sometimes we all just need a good bowl of tomato soup, a grilled cheese sandwich, and some ice cream. I believe whether someone is living with a terminal illness or not, people have to do the things that make them happy. If you need to treat yourself every now and then, do so.

Your body will go through a lot as it deals with cancer and cancer treatments, so try to give it your best shot. Your body is a machine, just like your car; it can't perform properly without the right fuel in the tank!

I did a lot of research on diet first, and then I asked my oncologist to give me a referral to a nutritionist. The diet I chose to follow was personalized for me and seems to have served me well.

CHAPTER 6 - GET MOVING

So next up, let's talk about exercise. Unless you've spent your life living in a cave, I'm pretty sure you've heard of the wonderful benefits that we get from regular exercise. It's a shame we all know of its importance, yet so many of us don't do it regularly. In case you are one of the non-consistent exercisers out there, hopefully, you'll decide it's time to start. If it's too much to take on something strenuous, start small by at least getting outside and going for a walk every day.

The American Heart Association recommends we get at least 150 minutes per week of moderate-intensity aerobic activity or 75 minutes per week of vigorous aerobic activity, or a combination of both preferably spread throughout the week.[11]

---

[11] American Heart Association, "American Heart Association Recommendations for Physical Activity in Adults and Kids," accessed April 15, 2022, https://www.heart.org/en/healthy-living/fitness/fitness-basics/aha-recs-for-physical-activity-in-adults

Exercising can improve memory and brain function in all age groups. It can protect against many chronic diseases. It aids in weight management. It lowers your blood pressure and improves heart health. It even improves your quality of sleep and increases your life span. [12] Still need more reasons?

Exercising improves joint pain and stiffness. It helps maintain muscle strength and balance. Most importantly for me, it combats cancer-related fatigue! All of these benefits have been scientifically proven, but from my firsthand experiences, I can say I wholeheartedly concur. I have been consistently exercising now for the past five years.

I don't think this is going to come as a surprise to you, but prior to my cancer diagnosis, other than walking and a weekly yoga class, the only exercise I really got was minimal. I was too busy working a full-time job and raising my children. I thought that was a good excuse for not being able to fit in exercise.

---

[12] American Heart Association, "American Heart Association Recommendations for Physical Activity in Adults and Kids," accessed April 15, 2022, https://www.heart.org/en/healthy-living/fitness/fitness-basics/aha-recs-for-physical-activity-in-adults

I don't believe that if I had become a steady fitness person sooner, I wouldn't have gotten cancer, but I can tell you, in retrospect, I could have had fewer aches and pains and much more energy. Currently, even when I feel awful, I exercise. It makes me not only feel better physically but mentally too. It almost sounds counterintuitive, but exercising when I feel fatigued makes me feel less tired and helps with my brain fog too. It also helps with the quality of my sleep.

As you already know, another big decision I made to help myself with my cancer journey was to join a cancer support group. Through this support group, I learned of a cancer wellness group. It is a nonprofit organization called Strength for Life. This cancer wellness group is located on Long Island in New York, and its programs are available to cancer patients and survivors free of charge.

I began by taking one exercise class a week. I then progressed to two a week, and before I knew it, I was up to three. I couldn't believe how great it made me feel!

In these classes, we are not training for marathons. Everyone honors themselves by going at their own pace, and we all say we feel better after we exercise. I never would have imagined that getting cancer would lead me to weekly yoga, tai chi, line dancing, strength training, stretching, toning, and nutrition and writing classes… All while giving me the opportunity to make so many new friends.

My body is in good shape, and my stamina is up, but sometimes there are days where I'm just not up to moving around - and that's okay. I've learned the importance of listening to my body. If it's telling me to take the day off, I do.

At the beginning of my nursing career, I worked in a general surgery unit. Back in those days, patients were admitted to hospitals more often and stayed for much longer periods of time. As patients recovered from their surgeries, strict bedrest was usually ordered for the first several days. Thank goodness the benefits of physical movement were realized, and a shift was made to get patients up and moving as quickly as possible after surgery. This happened for medical patients as well.

I have heard many cancer patients say they felt helpless during their cancer journeys, but that exercise helped them gain a sense of control. Obviously, there is a big mental component to exercising as well. If you can find some type of formal exercise program, I highly recommend you take advantage of it. In the event that's not possible, here is another suggestion.

At a cancer conference I recently attended, I received a copy of the book "Moving Through Cancer" by Kathryn Schmitz, Ph.D. [13] Dr. Schmitz is the director of the Oncology, Nutrition, and Exercise Group at the Penn State Cancer Institute. In her book, she tells the story of several of her patients but mainly focuses on her journey with her wife Sara, who was diagnosed with Stage 3 squamous cell carcinoma in her nose.

Not only does this author talk openly about the journey, but she teaches readers about programs they can follow before treatments begin, during therapy, throughout reconstruction, post-treatment, and for the rest of their life. Many major institutions and practitioners use her protocols for exercise in cancer care.

Research not only proves the benefits of movement/exercise for cancer patients but also supports how beneficial support groups are at reducing the 3 most

---

[13] Dr. Kathryn Schmitz, Penn State Cancer Institute, "Moving Through Cancer," Chronicle Prism 2021

significant stressors associated with cancer. These are unwanted aloneness, loss of control, and loss of hope. Start moving today and seek out the wellness groups in your area!

CHAPTER 7 – STEERING CLEAR OF TOXINS

In the cancer documentary "The C-Word – We Can Beat Cancer Before it Beats Us." Dr. Servan-Schreiber talks a lot about the chemical toxins that are all around us. In the world we live in today, total toxin avoidance is impossible. We can reduce our exposure to them by making conscious decisions to do so. Toxins are in the air we breathe, the water we drink, and the food we eat. They exist all around us. Chemicals like formaldehyde are in the products we use to build and furnish our homes. Toxic chemicals are even found in our personal care items, like makeup, soaps, shampoos, and the cleaners we use to clean our homes.

Along with the "artificial ingredients" and high contents of salt and sugar we've added to our foods, chemicals are added as well. Some of them are even known to cause cancer. We've all heard stories of how our foods in this country are preserved. This is done so that they can leave the farms (or the seas) and get to us, days and weeks later, in the supermarket, still looking pretty and smelling fresh. Eating organic foods, of course, is ideal, but they are very expensive. It's true that you can't put a price tag on good health, but believe me, I realize that buying "cleaner" foods and "cleaner" cleaning products can be very expensive.

Many of us admire beautiful, lush green, and weed-free lawns, but in order to have them, we apply chemicals that end up in our water supply. I am one of those lush green lawn, weed-free, loving people but poisoned water, no thank you. It's hard for me to wrap my head around this stuff.

Another thing that doesn't make sense to me is how many people still smoke cigarettes. Research has shown for years now that smoking CAUSES cancer. That fact is even printed on cigarette packaging. And back to the subject of expensive things, the cost of a pack of cigarettes in my neighborhood is up to ten dollars! If you smoke, you should really consider quitting. Believe me, I know it is not easy. Smoking is detrimental not only to your health but also to the health of those around you. If you are a smoker, people in your house or at your work become passive smokers.

Growing up, my mother and father smoked a lot in our home. After they divorced, they both remarried spouses who were heavy smokers too. My husband, when we first started dating, was also a smoker. Thankfully he was able to quit permanently when our first son was born.

I had never been a habitual smoker, but I did have a cigarette every once in a while. I was always in the company of so many smokers; therefore, a cigarette was never far away. I gave up smoking socially as soon as I became pregnant, and thankfully neither of our children has ever smoked.

Not only do we need to avoid environmental toxins where and when possible, but it's also important for us to learn to avoid toxic people. This is also a great way to manage your stress which will be covered in the next chapter.

Toxic is a pretty strong word to use to describe a person, but I'm sure you know at least one of these people. Toxic people are usually in your surroundings and possess more than their fair share of meanness, selfishness, jealousy, vindictiveness, and negativity. Being around people with these traits causes us to have stress. They usually only have their best interest at heart anyway. I think what makes being around toxic people even more difficult is that most of the time, they don't even realize that they are toxic in the first place.

Avoiding them is one way you can manage your stress. Again balance is important here. For some people, you will have to find new coping mechanisms not to let them "harsh your mellow," as my hippy friend always says. Setting boundaries and limiting your exposure to them is a good place to start. Remember this is necessary for your emotional health. Sometimes you will have to eliminate them from your life altogether. Walking away from them is not a sign of weakness; it's a sign of wisdom. There are some people who won't love you no matter what you do. I have a friend who loves to say, "Sometimes the weight you need to lose isn't on your body."

Get rid of the people in your life who are holding you down. Invest your time with positive people who don't suck the energy out of you. As I've heard Oprah Winfrey quoted, "Surround yourself with only people who are going to lift you higher." And stop spending lots of time with negative people or your own negative thoughts. Shift your mindset to find the good in your situation. – Have confidence in yourself. And most of all, love yourself.

Start turning your lemons into lemonades. Just remember, though, a rotten lemon is still a rotten lemon and will make an awful drink – so it's better to just get rid of the rotten ones altogether.

CHAPTER 8 – MANAGING STRESS

Stress is the feeling of being overwhelmed or unable to cope with mental or emotional pressure. Stress can be acute, episodic, or chronic. We've all heard of the fight-or-flight response, we as humans experience, when we're in stressful situations. The fight or flight response, or stress response, is triggered by a release of hormones either prompting us to stay and fight or run away.

It is so unhealthy to live with this heightened alert feeling all of the time. However, it is up to us to respond to those stress-heightening hormones in either way.

A little bit of stress for some is necessary and motivating. Some people need pressure, like a deadline, to help them get things done. This can be a good thing in a way. I know (and love) quite a few people that need the stress that waiting to the very last minute brings. I am not that person at all anymore. Currently, I am probably one of the calmest people I know. I've chosen not to experience stress at all now, even when I'm facing another big cancer treatment decision.

As you can guess, before my cancer diagnosis, I was someone who lived under self-induced, chronic stress ALL OF THE TIME. Going back to my original breast cancer diagnosis and its treatments, I told you I continued working throughout them. (It was a very stressful job too.) I wanted everything to seem "normal" in order to not upset anyone else. It would just worry my husband, sons, family members, and friends if they knew I was actually sick, or so I believed.

I thought it would make things harder on my coworkers if I missed work. They'd have to pick up my slack, and I didn't want them to. If the situation had been reversed, I wouldn't have hesitated to step up and take on some of their workloads.

From a very young age, I made the constant mistake of thinking I had to be all things, to all people, all of the time. Imagine how stressful that could be. So far, I have given my poor diet, lack of exercise, and long-standing exposure to cigarette smoke a pass, but now as I'm writing this, this one might be what I'd like to blame my cancer on! (Just kidding here… chronic stress is detrimental to your health, but it has not been proven that it causes cancer)

From a young age, although I was fairly shy, I was very likable and popular. I would never do anything that would upset someone. I realize now that people liked me as much as they did because I was the consummate people pleaser. I never wanted to argue with anyone or hurt someone's feelings. I always wanted to help make everyone's life easier, but in doing so, I lived always feeling so overwhelmed, AND of course, I kept this to myself. Saying the word "NO" was not part of my vocabulary. Taking time to take care of myself was something I would never consider. I needed to take care of everyone else.

I say now that I was like a duck gliding gracefully along the surface of the water, but underneath, I was paddling like hell. And the crazy thing is I did this to myself. And who cares about what a duck looks like anyway!

When I speak with people now about my past "mistakes," I tell them that I was always someone who was a great friend to others, but I was a terrible friend to myself. I was never truly happy until I started to treat myself the same way I treated people I loved. Makes a lot of sense, right?

Learning to say no to people is good. Learning to say exactly what you mean is essential. Learning to say yes to things that you really want is awesome. Learning to trust your instincts and to put yourself first is so important. It is for your own good. Don't overthink things so much. Trust that you made the right decision. Stop doubting yourself and be kind to yourself. Let go of what you can't control, and stay away from negativity and drama. Most of your stress comes from the way you respond, not the way life is. When you adjust your attitude, so much of the extra stress disappears.

Even without having to deal with a serious illness, life is hard enough. Bad relationships, financial problems, difficult children, elderly parents, horrible jobs, and just living life, in general, all cause stress. That is why it has to be "managed' if it can't be gotten rid of altogether.

I realize now that once I took control of what I could control and started letting go of what I couldn't, my life became easier. I came to the realization that in spite of my incurable illness, it was time to start living one day at a time, as fully as I could and without allowing stress any room in it.

If I do feel myself getting stressed about something now, I take one thought at a time and only one task at a time. This is quite difficult for many to do. If you haven't tried meditation, I recommend you try it. It can help you immensely.

Meditation is the practice of focused concentration that enables you to bring your thoughts back to the moment over and over again. It can help with stress and can also reduce anxiety, pain, depression, heart disease, and high blood pressure. Simple deep breathing, tai chi, and yoga can be utilized as calming techniques as well.

Another way to manage your stress is to spend more time around people who "get you." These people are known as your community, your tribe. They share the same interests and goals as you. They are a group that you share similar characteristics with. Sometimes your community can be your family members, a group of your friends, people in your religious circle, or even a structured support group.

All human beings need a sense of purpose: a reason to get up and out of bed every day. Think about what yours is. If you don't have one, I suggest you get one. If you do have one, do you live meaningfully and mindfully for it? If you don't, now is the time to start, assuming you're looking for a life you are happy to be living. I know you are dealing with cancer right now, but there is a lot more to you than your cancer.

CHAPTER 9 – BEING WHOLE

In nursing school, I remember learning about physical illnesses before we progressed to mental illnesses. I remember I enjoyed learning the physical curriculum, but the mental curriculum scared me. I could feel someone's hernia, see it on their radiological imaging and prepare them for surgery to have it repaired. Mental illness is not as straightforward. Minds are fragile. I can't actually see, feel, or touch mental wellness or mental illness.

When it came to spirituality, I think all I retained from my formal education on this topic was that people's religious affiliation mattered. It needed to be taken into consideration when we cared for them. Patients' religions were found on their charts and even on their hospital identification bracelets. I always knew to call the Religious Services Department when patients or their families requested we do so. Then clergy personnel would take it from there.

Now I understand human beings so much more. Body, mind, and spirit are not three separate areas that can be placed in their own silos. You can be one hundred percent well physically, but that's not going to serve you if you're broken mentally and/or spiritually.

I'm pretty sure we all understand what good physical health is, but I realize just how subjective this is. My husband laughs every time he is in a room with me, and he hears me tell a doctor, "You know, except for this metastatic breast cancer diagnosis, I'm pretty healthy." It sounds crazy, but I am in good health. I have tumors in several areas in my bones and liver, which do cause issues, but I am in my sixties with no other illness than breast cancer.

Most nights, I sleep well and wake up feeling rested. The first thing I do when I get up is go to the bathroom because my kidneys are functioning well. I get there independently. I have a fairly decent appetite with a healthy stomach and colon. I don't have diabetes, heart disease, kidney issues, breathing problems, or cognitive issues. The only box I check off when I fill out those medical forms is the cancer one. I think this qualifies me as pretty healthy.

Good mental health is characterized by a person's ability to perform several key functions and activities, including the ability to learn, feel, express, and manage a range of positive and negative emotions, and the ability to form and maintain good relationships with others. Thankfully my mental health was good prior to the cancer, but in retrospect, I now see it needed some tweaking too.

Before I had cancer, I used to spend more time dwelling on my negative thoughts. Funny enough, I always thought how horrible it would be if I got a really bad illness. Now here I am telling medical professionals what a healthy person I am! Our mind and how we use it has so much of an influence over us. I agree with the famous pastor Charles R. Swindoll when he says, "Life is ten percent what happens to you and 90 percent how you react to it."

Another great quote along this same line is one from Joyce Meyers, a famous Bible teacher. She says, "Being negative only makes the journey more difficult. You may be given a cactus, but you don't have to sit on it." Being negative also goes hand in hand with beating ourselves up. We already learned that it serves no purpose.

There is more to be learned to improve our mental health in this quote from Creig Crippen, which I just love. He says, "Forgive yourself for not knowing what you didn't know until you lived through it. Honor your path. Trust your journey. Learn, grow, evolve, become."

Now that I've already told you, I was in a fairly good physical and mental place before my cancer journey: this is the part where I talk about how my spirituality was lacking.

My brother, sister, and I were raised Catholic by our mom. My father had been raised Jewish. Our extended family was very religiously diverse. My dad had two sisters who were also raised Jewish. My one aunt married a Jewish man, and their children, my cousins, were Jewish. My father's other sister married a man who was a Seventh Day Adventist. She converted. They and their children were Seventh Day Adventists. My mother's brother married a Lutheran woman, so those first cousins were Lutheran.

It was great being exposed to an array of religious observances and ceremonies while I was growing up. After a while, I began to realize there were commonalities among them and some major differences. I reached the decision some time ago that a formal religion was not for me. Although I am not religious, I consider myself to be very spiritual.

I respect people who are strongly committed to their religion, especially after taking care of so many patients of every religion. One of my worst days working as a nurse was the day when a young patient of mine started to hemorrhage following her surgery. She was a Jehovah's Witness. This religion believes that another creature's blood cannot be used to prolong human life. For them, blood transfusions are not an option.

In an attempt to stop her bleeding and thicken her blood, some other alternatives were tried, but it was obvious she was not going to make it. Her physicians emphatically explained the gravity of the situation to her and her family and urged her to have her blood transfused. She did not consent to this, and she died.

Although this was tragic in my mind, it helped me realize how different human beings can be and that their beliefs belong to them. We all have to respect that about each other.

Over the years, I have come to know many people with such a strong faith in God, whether it's backed up by a formal religion or not. I also understand that there are plenty of people in this world who don't believe in God.

Spirituality doesn't just encompass one's religious beliefs. It is a higher state of consciousness and connection. Spiritual states are self-awareness, empathy, and your sense of connectedness. Just a few examples of how people feel this connection are through God, the universe, nature, music, love, Buddha, Allah, or yoga.

Earlier I had mentioned that I practice yoga. Yoga is beneficial not only physically and mentally but also spiritually. When I went to my first yoga class many years ago, I had no idea. The teacher started talking about my chakras and third eye, and I thought she was just a bit weird.

The more I stuck with my yoga practice, the more it helped me. In the beginning, I remember being so tense. Just sitting there quietly, cross-legged, and deep breathing helped me relax. I had lots of joint pain, and muscle aches, and those yoga poses really helped me get relief. However, this third eye part took some time for me to understand.

In yoga, the third eye is the site of the psychic chakra. A chakra is an energy point. This third eye is a mystical concept that centers on an invisible eye that elevates one's level of perception. A part of the subtle body, the third eye symbolizes higher consciousness. Opening the third eye promotes perception and supports spiritual insight. I don't think energy points and a third eye are weird any more.

Nature and music are other ways that provide me with feelings of well-being and connectedness. Nothing makes me feel better than getting outdoors for a walk. Walking alone is great; walking with friends is even better (two or four-legged ones). Music, for me can turn my whole day around. On my drive to all of my medical appointments, I blast the radio, and I sing loudly. Whenever I am in a situation where I need to muster up extra confidence and/or calmness, I either sing or repeat affirmations to myself.

I remind myself that I have gotten through so much already, and I know I can get through more. I have so much love around me. I have trust in myself and lots of hope. Good health just doesn't come from medicine for physical conditions. It comes from peace of mind, peace of heart, and peace of soul. It comes from laughter and being loved.

How great would it be if people went to their doctors when they weren't feeling well and were given the following recommendations? "Try spending more time outside and less indoors, stop worrying about the things you can't control, turn off your television, meditate every day, exercise for at least 30 minutes every day, and avoid processed foods. Make sure to eat more fruit and vegetables. Please come back to see me in three weeks". Instead of only hearing, "Take these pills twice a day."

In my opinion, this scenario represents the scenario we need to be experiencing more often. This is the kind of health care we get when traditional medicine is practiced in combination with integrative care. I'll speak more about that in the next chapter.

CHAPTER 10 – RESEARCH TRIALS, CHEMO PORTS, AND ALTERNATIVE MEDICINE

Along with your cancer diagnosis come decisions you will need to make in regard to how you're going to treat it. These decisions can be so difficult to make. Earlier in this book, I only spoke about conventional treatment options. Now it's time to discuss three other areas; clinical trials, Mediports, and integrative/alternative medicine.

I have always been a big believer in science and facts. I also am experienced enough to know how hard it is these days to actually find factual, non-biased information. In a capitalist society, people are in business to make money. Drug companies, hospitals, cancer centers, health care providers, and even health insurance companies fall under this umbrella. When/if greed is a factor in health care, it can make us skeptical about trusting the data and the conclusions that are drawn.

Without being political here, we need to realize "evidenced based practice" is still the reasonable approach to follow in regard to how medical care is practiced. There are a lot of people out there advertising and rendering unproven treatments – Be careful.

That being said, unproven is not the same as non-conventional or non-traditional. It's difficult to directly compare non-conventional therapies with conventional ones, but that doesn't mean though that all unproven remedies are useless. Right now, a lot of research is being done to test the effectiveness of Complementary and Alternative Medicine.

In Nursing School, I remember learning about clinical trials/clinical research and the necessary requirements it took for drugs and medical treatments to be approved in America. Under the auspices of the FDA, this process is often a long, tedious one. Before medications and other medical treatments can be available for providers to prescribe to patients, safety and efficacy must be proven.

In 2015 working as a Nurse in the Quality Improvement arena, I was directly involved with a national nursing research project. It was very enlightening to be on that side of the fence. As a cancer patient, I have been a participant in three clinical trials.

Participating in a clinical trial is a very interesting experience. Some trials are set up so that a group of participants will get the "trial" treatment while others will get the already approved standard treatment or a placebo. (Placebos will never be used in cases of advanced cancers.) Sometimes it is not the drug's effectiveness that is being studied but which dosage is most beneficial.

The clinical trial process is designed to ensure that new treatments are better than existing treatments and progress through phases. Treatments move through the phases, but patients do not, and most of the time, if you take part in a clinical trial, you will only be in that one phase of the study.

There are two reasons I say yes to participating in clinical trials. Firstly, I feel obligated to help science and future cancer patients, and secondly, I hope that what's being "trialed" will benefit me. Of course, like many things in life, there are risks involved and no guarantees, but I'm glad I elected to participate.

Over the past 6 years, I have been on 9 different courses of chemotherapies. Some of the drugs which have worked temporarily to slow down my disease's progression weren't even available when I was initially diagnosed with breast cancer in 2010. Thank goodness scientists, researchers, and drug companies have made the advances they have, but there is still a long way to go.

If you think you would be interested in a clinical trial, speak to your doctor about it. It is possible your doctor may suggest them to you as well. A great source for information about clinical trials and a list of every ongoing trial worldwide is on the National Cancer Institute's website at www.clinicaltrials.gov. This site can be a bit confusing to navigate for some people. Another place where you can find information on cancer clinical trials is from the Cancer Support Community's Clinical Trial Matching Service at www.cancersupportcommunity.com.

I think it's safe to say we can all agree the American Health Care System has many shortcomings. The biggest one, in my opinion, is that we spend way too much money and effort fighting disease and not enough on preventing it. I have seen a shift during my years spent in health care with patients now being treated with their whole being considered instead of just focusing on their illness. That is the mission at many cancer centers where integrative care is now incorporated.

Integrative medicine is an approach to medical care that combines conventional medicine with patients' preferences and attempts to address health's mental, physical, and spiritual aspects. This type of care may be called complementary, integrative, or alternative medicine. It is usually used together with mainstream medical care.

According to the NIH/National Cancer Institute, Complementary and Alternative Medicine (CAM) is the term for medical products and practices that are not part of standard medical care. People with cancer may use CAM to help cope with the side effects of cancer treatment, such as nausea, pain, and fatigue. They can use these techniques for several reasons. For example, to give themselves comfort, or ease the worries of cancer treatment and related stress, to feel they are doing something to help with their own care and/or try to treat or cure their cancer.

Types of CAM can be mind-body therapies, biologically based practices, manipulative and body practices, energy healing, or whole medical systems. Mind-body therapies are therapies that combine mental focus, breathing, and body movement to help relax the body and mind. Meditation, biofeedback, yoga, hypnosis, imagery, and tai chi are all examples of mind-body therapies.

Biologically based practices are another form of CAM. This type of Complementary and Alternative Medicine uses things found in nature such as vitamins, dietary supplements, botanicals like cannabis and medicinal mushrooms, or herbs and spices.

Another form of CAM is manipulative and body practices. These are based on working with one or more parts of the body like massage therapy, chiropractic therapy, or reflexology. Several years ago, I sought out the help of a physical therapist certified in Myofascial Release to help me with horrible shoulder pain. Myofascial release is similar to massage, but it's different. Massage works with soft tissue and the overall system of muscles in the body to relieve stress and tension, but myofascial release works specifically with the connective tissue to relieve the tightness that causes muscle restrictions.

Energy healing is also a type of CAM and is based on the belief that vital energy flows through the body. Reiki and therapeutic touch are examples of this. Currently, according to the NCI, there is not enough evidence to support the existence of energy fields, but there are no harmful effects documented in using these approaches.

Whole medical systems are also a type of CAM. Whole medical systems are healing systems and beliefs that have evolved over time in different parts of the world. Traditional Chinese medicine, naturopathic medicine, and Ayurvedic medicine are 3 examples of whole medical systems.

Ayurvedic medicine is a system from India in which the goal is to cleanse the body and restore balance to the body, mind, and spirit. It uses diet, herbal medicines, exercise, meditation breathing, physical therapy, and other methods.

Traditional Chinese medicine is based on the belief that the body's energy flows through channels in the body and keeps a person's spiritual, emotional, mental, and physical health in balance. It aims to restore and keep the body's balance between yin and yang forces. Acupuncture is a common practice in Chinese medicine that involves stimulating certain points in the body to promote health or to lessen disease symptoms and treatment side effects. I have heard many cancer patients speak so highly regarding acupuncture and the benefits they get in relieving their anxiety, pain, nausea, and even constipation.

Naturopathic medicine is a medical system that avoids drugs and surgery. It is based on the use of natural agents such as air, water, light, heat, and massage to help the body heal itself if may also use herbal products, nutrition, acupuncture, and aromatherapy.

You already know the complimentary things I use. Complementary medicine is used along with standard treatment, but it is not considered by itself to be standard treatment. If you are considering using CAM, you should talk with your doctor about it. Sometimes methods that appear to be safe can be harmful or interfere with standard medical treatments.

Before I began writing this book, I thought long and hard about everything I would have liked to have known when I was initially diagnosed with cancer. That's why I feel compelled to add something about ports and how much in favor I am of them now. I wasn't too fond of the idea of having one at first.

A chemo port also called a Mediport, PowerPort, or implanted port, is a small medical appliance that is surgically installed and remains beneath the skin. Implanted ports are made up of two pieces. One is a small disc made of plastic or metal with a rubber seal at the top, and the other is a small, plastic flexible tube called the catheter. The disc is usually the size of a nickel or quarter and can be round, oval, or triangular.

One end of the catheter is connected to the port, and the other end sits in a large vein near your heart. It's usually tender for a few days after the port is inserted initially, but it can be used immediately once it's in.

The doctor places ports in a sterile environment such as the operating room or interventional radiology area. Under local anesthetic, the doctor makes 2 small cuts, one on the chest below the collarbone and one at the base of the neck for the catheter. The lump created from the disc will be noticeable to the eye and felt under the skin.

When the port is "accessed," medicine, blood products, nutrients or fluids can be delivered into the bloodstream. Blood samples for patients' laboratory blood testing can also be collected from ports. Only trained licensed healthcare professionals (usually Registered Nurses) are allowed to "access" ports. In order for the port to be used, the nurse punctures the patient's skin to place a needle attached to IV tubing into the disc. (If it does hurt, it is just for a second.) This area will then be covered with a see-through bandage to make sure it stays protected from germs and in place.

When the medications or fluids are done being administered, the nurse flushes the port, removes the bandage, and then pulls the needle back out. Implanted ports can stay in place for years but will be removed when the patient doesn't need them anymore. I was very frightened of the thought of having a port, and I'm not sure why. It seems to me most people are as well. Once I had mine inserted, I was sorry I hadn't gotten it sooner.

As far as making cancer treatment decisions, patients must consider how their quality of life will be affected. Some side effects and adverse occurrences experienced from treatments can be just as bad as problems that arise from having cancer. If the side effect(s) is only temporary and the benefit obtained is positive, then I think it's a simpler decision to make. But some adverse effects can just be awful. Remember, not only are there no guarantees here, but there is also no way of knowing for certain how things will turn out for us. What works so well for one patient could severely harm another.

CHAPTER 11 – IT'S OKAY TO TALK ABOUT DEATH

Thinking and talking about death for most people is so difficult, and I wish that wasn't so. We are ALL going to die one day. If we use science to explain the process, it seems a little more palatable to me. Once our lungs and heart permanently cease to function, we are clinically dead. It is heart breaking for the loved ones left behind.

For the past five years, I have lived one day at a time and only focused on the present. It is still comforting to know that my doctor, in light of my incurable illness, is still checking off the greater than 6 month's prognosis box in my medical record. More importantly, most of the time, I feel well, and my good days still outnumber my bad ones. I won't be happy when this changes, but I have noticed that once I started living more wisely, I began to become less fearful of my death.

Four years ago, I was asked by one of the Social Workers at my cancer center if I would be interested in participating in a one-evening program they were going to be having. The program was called *"Death over Dinner,"* and boy, was I fortunate to have been asked to be a part of it.

Michael Hebb cofounded *Death over Dinner,* which is an organization that encourages people to "pull up a chair, break bread, and really talk about the one thing we all have in common." The website for this organization is listed in the resource guide, and I highly recommend his book titled, *Let's Talk about Death over Dinner.*

Michael received his inspiration to start this end-of-life awareness campaign based on his experience with his own father and after hearing countless stories from people who regretted not having conversations with their loved ones on this subject.

We need to be having critical conversations about death even when we are 100% healthy. Our loved ones should know more than just our practical considerations like Do Not Resuscitate wishes and where our will is, but also things like what we fear, what we hope for, and how we want to be remembered... And we should also know theirs. Sitting down to dinner to intentionally discuss death is exactly what Michael Hebb's program teaches people to do.

Since I already mentioned I like to say "yes" to things I told the Social Worker I would love to attend. There were a mixed group of invitees, but most of them were staff members of the cancer center. (Only four of us were actually patients.) We were separated into six groups, with eight of us at each table. We were served a very nice meal with a glass of beer or wine.

The facilitators gave us different topics to discuss at our table for sixty minutes. After that, all six groups gathered together to share their experiences. I was actually shocked to hear that most of the participants, who were physicians or nurses employed by a cancer center, had never had any death discussions with their loved ones. They all said either they or their partners found it too difficult to do. Interestingly enough, I and the three other cancer patients all had the jump on them!

When someone younger dies suddenly of a heart attack or in an accident, it is most likely they never took the opportunity to prepare for their death. Loved ones left behind are not only grief-stricken, but they are also in a state of shock because the death was so unexpected. It's extra hard for the deceased family members to figure out what the "final arrangements" should be because, most likely, they were never discussed. People who have lingering illnesses have a different set of issues, but they usually have opportunities to prepare for their death. They were afforded time to get their things in order, but that doesn't always mean they want to face these decisions, either.

I know plenty of advanced cancer patients who have a hard time wrapping their heads around the fact that they are going to die from their terminal disease... Believe me, I do understand it. It's very sad. I have intentionally used my incurable illness to my advantage and have made all of my "final arrangements" and wishes known to my family. Even as to the music to play at my funeral.

What I really want people to remember most about me when I'm gone are two things: 1) how much fun I had because I was actively living and 2) how much it meant to me to help motivate and inspire others, even while struggling with my own issues. What is the legacy you want to leave for your loved ones? In my opinion, it's never too late or too early to start working on it.

In chapter 4, I briefly mentioned the difference between palliative care and hospice care. In Merriam- Webster Dictionary, the medical definition of hospice "is a facility or program designed to provide palliative care and emotional support to the terminally ill in a home or homelike setting so that quality of life is maintained and family members may be active participants in care."

Hospice starts when doctors estimate a patient only has six months to live. This determination is usually made by a hospice physician and the patient's primary or specialist physician. Once patients choose to receive hospice care, it doesn't mean they are giving up. It's also important to know that people who use hospice care don't die faster.

Since this is such an emotional and important topic, I reached out to a peer who has been a hospice nurse for 35 years, both in the state of New York and Florida. (State regulations governing hospice vary a little, but overall, the hospice premise is the same in all 50 states.) Often people view hospice as a death sentence. She told me that the hospice team could not help patients receive more quantity of time, but they do provide quality to the time they have left.

With hospice, patients can remain in their homes or eventually go to a hospice unit/facility. The hospice team can include the doctor, nurse, a social worker, and even Home Health Aides to help with bathing and other personal care tasks. As patients become frailer and closer to their deaths, the more frequent the team visits become.

Hospice care addresses all symptoms of a disease but has a special focus on controlling discomfort and pain. It provides comfort and support to both patients and families. Loved ones can benefit by having hospice professionals on call 24 hours, seven days a week, and they won't need to be inconvenienced taking the patient out of the home. Another added benefit to hospice is that the family receives guidance, support, and grief counseling.

Death and dying are a part of life, and everyone's experience with it is unique. So, I just wanted to talk about one last thing on this subject. I live in the state of New York, which is not a state that has authorized any medical aid in dying laws. I find this is really another subject people could use some education on.

The first state to allow this was Oregon in 1997. There are now eight states and Washington D.C. that have passed the death with dignity laws. In these places, the laws make it legal for adults with terminal illnesses to receive prescription medication that assists in their death. This is also known as physician-assisted suicide. Of course, patients must meet several conditions, and there are safeguards in place that go along with these laws to prevent misuse.

Physician-assisted suicide is only allowed for mentally competent adults who have been given six months or less to live because of a terminal illness. This means death must be inevitable for a person to receive the medications that will end their pain and suffering. Of course, this is a very controversial topic and has been debated throughout the nation.

Some people believe that this is a person's right to choose and that the government should not be allowed to dictate how someone ends their own life. Conversely, some religious leaders feel these laws should be repealed because they believe suicide is a sin. This is so controversial that provider participation with these laws is strictly voluntary.

Any physician licensed to practice in a "death with dignity state" is allowed to participate if they agree. The laws also say every physician has the choice not to participate. Two physicians are required in order for a patient to do this. If a patient is a candidate, one doctor will guide them through the requirements of the law and write the life-ending medication prescription, while the second doctor will certify all the criteria of the law have been met.

Once the patient has gotten the medication, they can self-administer and ingest it at a place of their choosing, although it cannot be in a public place. It is up to the patient when they take them. Some people know when the time is right because they've reached a point where their disease and/or pain and suffering no longer allow them an acceptable quality of life. It is interesting to know that about 30 percent of the patients never take the medication but simply knowing they have this option, if they need it, gives them comfort.[14]

I remember years and years ago first learning about Murad Jacob "Jack" Kevorkian for the first time. He was a pathologist and euthanasia proponent who championed a terminal patient's right to die by physician-assisted suicide. I had mixed emotions about this all the way back then, and I still do. I have witnessed our pets being euthanatized, and it always seemed like a peaceful experience for them. On the other hand, I've also taken care of some patients with very long, drawn-out agonizing deaths.

In the case of terminally ill people who can choose to swallow pills knowing their death will occur within hours, I admire them for the courage it takes for such a choice. I

---

[14] Death With Dignity, "Frequently Asked Questions", accessed on April 14, 2022, https://deathwithdignity.org/resources/faqs/

know someone who had a terminally ill sister who chose to use this end-of-life option. She had a hard time wrapping her head around the fact that this was what her sister did. I consoled her by saying that it was her sister's choice to hasten her imminent death, and it was done in a peaceful, humane, and dignified manner. Every ones' choices have to be respected.

CHAPTER 12 – THE NEW NORMAL

From my time spent around so many people who have dealt firsthand with cancer, I would say receiving a cancer diagnosis for most people is life-changing. It does not matter what type of cancer or stage it is. Not everyone joins a cancer support group. Some people I've met over the years didn't want to discuss anything about their cancer. I think the reason people have trouble dealing with cancer is that they are fearful of the uncertainty that comes with it. That's very understandable if you ask me!

When people spend time with me, I don't want them to say things to make me feel better about having cancer. Cancer patients hear some of the craziest things from the people around them. I feel people mean well when they say things to cancer patients like, "At least you're lucky they caught it early" or "Oh, so you have the good kind of cancer." As an MBC patient, I know that the question that bothers me the most is when people ask, "when will I be finished with my treatments?" It's not their fault that they don't understand my cancer. I always tell them that my treatments will stop when there are no more treatments left to give me.

Sometimes people who don't have cancer try to talk us out of how we are feeling. This can make us feel like what we are going through is being minimized. I also don't need to be reminded of all the good things I have in my life. I already know that, and I am grateful.

I am a person who is living with cancer. I possess a positive attitude on most days, but that doesn't mean there aren't days where I feel awful, physically and mentally. At times I have been mad, sad, and fearful all at the same time. I have had some chemo treatments that kicked my butt and medication side effects that were awful. Even without cancer, people go through bad days, which is okay. Many cancer patients have said, "Sometimes I need a good pity party, but I don't let it last too long." I get that!

A few years ago, this commercial for a metastatic breast cancer medication was on television. It portrayed "Carla" and her "new normal." At first, I couldn't stand this commercial, but now I can relate to it. Actually, in retrospect, I think it was even a decent commercial, as far as those drug commercials go. Apparently, Carla was initially thrown by her diagnosis, but before long, she was able to resume being Carla, just with a "new normal." I have to say life for me now is mostly normal, but with the exceptional bad days, it's better. There are a few reasons why.

I had already mentioned that when I first had to deal with cancer, I didn't really spend much time dwelling on it. I continued working through the whole surgery, chemo, and radiation ordeals. When I first lost my hair, I bought a wig that closely resembled the hairstyle I always had. Through an amazing organization called *Look Good, Feel Better,* I learned how to apply makeup, draw on fake eyebrows and apply false eyelashes. I believe I did very well, appearing that everything was "just fine." I didn't let many people know about what I was going through. I was on a mission to preserve my "normality" and put cancer behind me.

Once I was diagnosed with MBC, things were totally different. This time I needed to talk about what I was going through. I became more honest with other people and myself. I told my husband and family that if I wasn't going to get a lot more tomorrows, I wanted to start fully living every day. In order to really enjoy living, I realized I would need to start saying yes more often. Yes, to things like trips, walks on the beach, hikes, spending time with people I love, better sleep, healthier eating, and more fun. I also knew I would need to learn the art of saying no. No to things I didn't want to do or things that didn't serve me well.

I also needed to learn how to not take myself so seriously. I really do love to laugh, and sometimes I laugh hardest at myself. (Laughter is really good medicine!) I also wanted to start living actively, with intent, and not by habit.

I became an active volunteer with the American Cancer Society. I fundraise for them and speak at different types of events. Helping them with their endeavors also helps me. I am honored that it is my face that people get to see as they listen to my story about a woman living with advanced breast cancer. I've been on television, radio, and podcasts for them. I even spoke at one of their events in front of an audience of nine hundred people.

The American Cancer Society is an amazing cancer resource. Most people know about their cancer research efforts but they do so much more. They are an organization dedicated to eliminating cancer. If you have cancer questions, you can reach a live person twenty-four hours a day, seven days a week. Please check out their website www.cancer.org. You may even be surprised to learn about all the patient programs and services they offer.

If you're not doing okay on your journey, it's important to tell your doctor if you have feelings of depression and emotional distress. Your healthcare team is there to help you cope with your feelings. Getting treated for depression, if necessary, may make a huge difference in the quality of your life.

CHAPTER 13 – FORGING AHEAD WITH RESILIENCE, HUMOR, AND GRIT

The subject of cancer is not a very glamorous one, but I hope this book was able to help you. I thought it was important to close by talking about resilience, humor, and grit. When dealing with cancer, having these three things on your side is helpful!

About six months into working as a new nurse, I received a new patient who was being admitted on a surgical unit. He was in his sixties, had a very sweet face, and a most pleasant demeanor. (I remember when I first saw him that he looked just like a leprechaun.)

He arrived in his own wheelchair and was there for an upcoming surgery. After the Nursing Assistant and I helped him to bed, but before I started asking him the litany of required questions, he asked if we wouldn't mind helping him. He then proceeded to remove his artificial leg and requested we put it in the closet. Next, he asked for a denture cup since he would need to remove his entire set of artificial teeth before bed. As the aide returned with the denture cup, he told me he would need something to put his hearing aide devices in and a container for his glass eye. For a second, it felt like he was playing a joke on us, but he was legit. He then went on to answer the questions I needed to ask him. His medical history seemed like it included every problem on the list.

A few days later, I was his assigned nurse again. His surgery had gone well, and he was happy he was going to be discharged home the following day. I remember remarking to him that I thought he was pretty amazing. I didn't often have patients who were as upbeat as him, especially with the number of problems he had. He went on to tell me that many good things had happened in his life, as well as many bad things. He said that even though he was not in control of them, he realized he always possessed the freedom to choose his attitude, given the circumstances. He didn't become what happened to him, his illnesses or disabilities, but instead was the man he wanted to be.

Drawing on my 35 years of nursing experiences, I tell people considering entering the nursing field now that I feel the two assets most beneficial to possess for this career are flexibility and adaptability. (Compassion is a huge plus too!) Now that I am writing this book, I believe they are wonderful traits to get you through any career and life.

Life throws many things at us; no one goes through it, just being handed roses. I think it serves us all well when we let go of the picture, we thought life would be like and learn to find joy in the story we are actually living. And if we don't like how we're living it, we need to make the necessary changes.

Getting back to my patient's story, how come some people roll with the punches so much better than others? I think we can agree here that this man's philosophy and ability to still see the glass as half full exemplify resilience and grit. What exactly is resilience? What exactly is grit?

Resilience is the ability to withstand adversity and bounce back from difficult life events. Being resilient does not mean that you won't experience stress, emotional upheaval, or suffering. Resilient people tap into their strengths and support systems to overcome challenges and work through problems.

Grit is a personality trait possessed by individuals who demonstrate passion and perseverance toward a goal, even when confronted by significant obstacles and distractions. Those who possess grit are able to self-regulate themselves and postpone their need for positive reinforcement.

When people comment that they are impressed by how well I've dealt with my cancer, I tell them that I'm well aware I am only getting one chance at my life, and I'm giving it my best shot.

My cancer journey has made me more sensitive. Not like "you hurt my feelings" sensitive. I just feel and care so much more deeply. When I read the obituaries, I usually say softly, but out loud to no one in particular, "I'm so sorry you died." When I hear of someone's passing on the news, especially a younger person or a cancer patient, it takes me a few minutes to come back into my own thoughts. I feel empathy for what the cancer patient probably went through, and I feel sympathy that the younger person wasn't able to get the number of years that I've gotten.

A few months ago, when I heard Norm McDonald passed away due to leukemia, that's how I felt. To me, he seemed like he was a really good guy, we were the same age, and I grew up adoring him. (Not to mention, he was a very funny man.) A few weeks after his death, I was reading a magazine article and learned he had made this joke ten years before his own death from cancer. He said it was wrong to say someone "lost their battle" with cancer when they died. He said, "I'm not a doctor, but I'm pretty sure that when you die, cancer also dies at exactly the same time. That, to me, is not a loss. That's a draw."

Life is a series of wins, losses, and draws. This whole cancer journey for me has been quite a ride. I truly am happy my life has turned out exactly the way it was supposed to. I know that with all that has happened to me in my past, I can confidently face my future, however long that may be.

In closing, there is just one more quote that really resonates with me, and I'd like to share it. It is unknown who said it. "Cancer may rob you of the blissful ignorance that once led you to believe that tomorrow stretched forever. In exchange, you are granted the vision of seeing each day as a precious gift to be used richly and wisely." Be hopeful, be grateful, live wisely, and laugh often!

CHAPTER 14 - CANCER RESOURCES

This is a list of online cancer resources where you can find help and information. Some of them I have spoken about in this book. There are others available, and many cancer-specific organizations are also helpful. If you conduct your own search, make sure to utilize reputable sources. Ask your providers or social work/patient advocate staff at your cancer center for their list(s). They can also provide you with listings of local cancer organizations and support/wellness groups. Also, for more information visit my website at www.alongcamecancer.org

American Cancer Society (ACS) www.cancer.org

American Society of Clinical Oncology www.asco.org

Association of Cancer Online Resources (ACOR) www.acor.org

CancerCare www.cancercare.org

CancerCompass www.cancercompass.com

Cancer Information from the American Society of Clinical Oncology (ASCO) www.cancer.net

Cancer Hope Network www.cancerhopenetwork.org

Cancer Links www.cancerlinks.org

Cancer News on the Net www.cancernews.com

Cancer Support Community www.cancersupportcommunity.org

Cancer Wellness Center www.cancerwellness.org

ClinicalTrials.gov ww.clinicaltrials.gov

LIVESTRONG www.livestrong.org

Look Good, Feel Better www.lookgoodfeelbetter.org

National Cancer Institute (NCI) www.cancer.gov

National Coalition for Cancer Survivorship (NCCS)
www.canceradvocacy.org

National Comprehensive Cancer Network (NCCN)
www.nccn.org

OncoLink www.oncolink.com

On Top of Cancer www.preventcancer.org

Patient Advocate Foundation (PAF)
www.patientadvocate.org

Patient Power   www.patientpower.info

Prevent Cancer Foundation (PCF) www.preventcancer.org

Strength For Life www.strengthforlifeny.org

U.S. National Library of Medicine: Medline Plus
www.medlineplus.gov

CANCER COMMUNITIES - CANCER SPECIFIC

Breast Cancer.org www.breastcancer.org

Colorectal Cancer Alliance www.ccalliance.org

Head and Neck Cancer Alliance www.headandneck.org

Living Beyond Breast Cancer www.lbbc.org

Lung Cancer Research Foundation
www.lungcancerresearchfoundation.org

Prostate Cancer Foundation www.pcf.org

ThyCa: Thyroid Cancer Survivors Association Inc
www.thyca.org